A New
Mum's
Special
Gift

Catherine Butcher

For a list of National Distributors visit www.cwr.org.uk

Unless otherwise indicated, all Scripture references are from the Holy Bible: New
International Version (NIV), copyright © 1973, 1978, 1984 by the International Bible
Society.

Other versions used:
CEV: Contemporary English Version, copyright © 1995 by American Bible Society.
Holman Christian Standard Bible, copyright © 1999, 2000, 2002, 2003 by Holman
Bible Publishers. NLT: New Living Translation, copyright © NLT: Holy Bible New
Living Translation, c 1996. Used by permission of Tyndale House Publishers Inc. *The
Message*: Scripture taken from *The Message*. Copyright © 1993, 1994, 1995, 1996,
2000, 2001, 2002. Used by permission of NavPress Publishing Group.

Concept development, editing, design and production by CWR

Cover image: Getty Images/Iconica/Tom Grill

The images on pages 8, 38, 52, 56, 63, 66 and 100 are from www.istockphoto.com
The images on pages 12, 17, 28, 36 and 104 are courtesy of Melanie Ray
The images on pages 24, 47, 83 and 88 are from www.123rf.com
The image on page 109 is from Image Source

Printed in China by 1010 Printing International Ltd.

ISBN: 978-1-85345-547-6

Contents

Introduction

Motherhood changes women forever. There's no going back. Even when your child is grown up, you will still be 'Mum'. As well as the obvious physical changes, motherhood takes us through the whole range of changing emotions: fierce love, chest-bursting pride and, sometimes, heart-breaking pain.

We change spiritually, too. By giving birth we take part in the ultimate creative process – the giving of life. We are given a crash course in learning to love unconditionally, without knowing the outcome, from God who loves without limits. We begin building a family, following God's lead – He has been inviting people to join His family since time began. And from the trusting and dependent baby in our arms we learn what Jesus meant when

He said: 'Unless you accept God's kingdom in the simplicity of a child, you'll never get in' (Luke 18:17, *The Message*).

Motherhood offers fresh insights into the heart of our Creator God who loves us and longs for us to be part of His family. Expect to find treasures, fresh insights and inexplicable strength, even in the darkest times. Make the most of every moment to discover more about yourself and God, as you build a new relationship with the precious child – this special gift – He has given into your care.

Thanks

∽∞∽

Gratitude

Blessed

*With all my heart I praise the Lord,
and I am glad because of God
   my Saviour.
He cares for me, his humble servant.
From now on, all people will say
   God has blessed me.
God All-Powerful has done great things
   for me …*

Luke 1:46–49, CEV

Mary's life changed forever when she became Jesus' mother. This is how Mary expressed her gratitude to God over the birth of Jesus. Her song of praise is often called *The Magnificat*.

The same All-Powerful God cares for you and your baby. He is ready to do great things for you, to bless you and your child. Express your gratitude to God in your own words.

Protected

*You, L*ORD*, brought me safely*
  through birth,
and you protected me when I was a
  baby at my mother's breast.
From the day I was born, I have been
  in your care,
and from the time of my birth,
  you have been my God.

Psalm 22:9–10, CEV

Thank God that this is true.
God is your protector.

Thank God for His presence throughout
your pregnancy and the birth of your child.

Make these psalms prayers for yourself
and then for your baby.

I depend on you,
and I have trusted you
since I was young.
I have relied on you from the day I
*   was born.*
You brought me safely
through birth,
and I always praise you.

Psalm 71:5–6, CEV

11

Chosen

Even before he made the world, God loved us and chose us in Christ to be holy and without fault in his eyes. God decided in advance to adopt us into his own family by bringing us to himself through Jesus Christ … it gave him great pleasure. So we praise God …

Ephesians 1:4–6, NLT

Next time your child is asleep in your arms, think about these verses opposite. Although there are times when loving is tough, most mums instinctively love their children. Marvel at the fact that God has chosen to love you – and your baby. He adopts Jesus' followers into His family. Because of Jesus, God sees you as faultless. His love is limitless.

13

Thankful

These prayers are used in the Church of England's 'Service of Thanksgiving for the Gift of a Child':

God our creator,
we thank you for the wonder of new life
and for the mystery of human love.
We thank you for all whose support
  and skill
surround and sustain the beginning of life.
We thank you that we are known to you
  by name
and loved by you from all eternity.
We thank you for Jesus Christ
who has opened to us the way of love.
We praise you, Father, Son, and
  Holy Spirit.

Common Worship:
'Thanksgiving for the Gift of a Child'[1]

14

If possible, pray this prayer with your baby's dad, a grandparent or a godparent who will share in your child's care:

God our creator,
we thank you for the gift of these
  children,
entrusted to our care.
May we be patient and understanding,
ready to guide and to forgive,
so that through our love
they may come to know your love;
through Jesus Christ our Lord.
Amen.

Common Worship: 'Thanksgiving for the Gift of a Child'[2]

Joy

Wonderful

God, brilliant Lord, yours is a
household name.
Nursing infants gurgle choruses
 about you;
toddlers shout the songs
That drown out enemy talk,
and silence atheist babble.
I look up at your macro-skies,
 dark and enormous,
your handmade sky-jewelry,
Moon and stars mounted in their
 settings.
Then I look at my micro-self and
 wonder,
Why do you bother with us?
Why take a second look our way?

Psalm 8:1–4, *The Message*

Many first-time parents realise there must be a Creator when their baby is born. As you look at the intricate way in which your child has been made, give thanks to God for His amazing creativity.

Singing and dancing

You did it: you changed wild
* lament*
into whirling dance;
You ripped off my black
* mourning band*
and decked me with wildflowers.
I'm about to burst with song;
I can't keep quiet about you.
God, my God,
I can't thank you enough.

Psalm 30:11–12, *The Message*

18

There are times in pregnancies and during labour when pain is more real than the promise of new life. After giving birth, holding a new baby usually brings a new joyful perspective.

Use this psalm to talk to God about how you feel.

(You might find Psalm 18 helpful if you went through a particularly difficult labour.)

The greatest

Hymn-writer Henry Jackson van Dyke (1852–1933), an English literature professor and church leader, wrote: 'There is a loftier ambition than merely to stand high in the world. It is to stoop down and lift mankind a little higher.'

Mothers rarely consider ourselves of high standing: 'I'm *just* a mum'. But in the topsy-turvy kingdom of God, a mother's role is among the greatest.

Joyful, joyful, we adore Thee,
  God of glory, Lord of love;
Hearts unfold like flowers before Thee,
  opening to the sun above.
Melt the clouds of sin and sadness;
  drive the dark of doubt away;
Giver of immortal gladness,
  fill us with the light of day!

Henry Jackson van Dyke, 1852–1933

The hand that rocks the cradle rules the world.

Mary Sumner, founder of Mothers' Union

21

Essential routines

Give thanks to the Lord, for he is good;
his love endures for ever.

Psalm 118:1, NIV

For health and strength and daily food
We praise your name, O Lord.

A traditional mealtime grace

Motherhood has a very humanising effect.
Everything gets reduced to essentials.

Meryl Streep, actress

Bring the essentials to God in prayer regularly and often – when you wake (or are woken by your baby!); when you eat or your child is feeding; washing, dressing, changing; – take every opportunity to rejoice and thank God out loud for all He has given.

Enable your child to grow a grateful heart as well as a strong body.

Rejoice in the Lord always. I will say it again: Rejoice! Let your gentleness be evident to all. The Lord is near. Do not be anxious about anything, but in everything, by prayer and petition, with thanksgiving, present your requests to God. And the peace of God, which transcends all understanding, will guard your hearts and your minds in Christ Jesus.

Philippians 4:4–7, NIV

Wonder

Be amazed . . .

. . . babies are pivotal to God's plan to rescue humanity.

*How inexplicable
that God would place
the salvation of the world
as an infant
in the arms
of two inexperienced parents.*

Anne E. Kitch[3]

And when I think that God,
  his Son not sparing,
sent him to die – I scarce can
  take it in
that on the cross,
  our burden gladly bearing,
he bled and died to take away
  our sin ...

tr. Stuart K. Hine, 1899–1989

Be ready to learn

Your baby relies on you for everything.
Allow your baby to teach you what Jesus
meant when He took a child and said:

*If you don't change and become like a
child, you will never get into the kingdom
of heaven. But if you are as humble
as this child, you are the greatest in
the kingdom of heaven. And when you
welcome one of these children because
of me, you welcome me.*

Matthew 18:3–5, CEV

26

God saved you by his grace when you believed. And you can't take credit for this; it is a gift from God. Salvation is not a reward for the good things we have done, so none of us can boast about it. For we are God's masterpiece. He has created us anew in Christ Jesus, so we can do the good things he planned for us long ago.

Ephesians 2:8–10, NLT

27

Wonder at God's care

Praise God, the Father of our Lord Jesus Christ! The Father is a merciful God, who always gives us comfort. He comforts us when we are in trouble, so that we can share that same comfort with others in trouble.

2 Corinthians 1:3–4, CEV

The Lord is like a father to his children
tender and compassionate to those
 who fear him.
For he knows how weak we are;
... The wind blows, and we are gone–
... But the love of the Lord remains
 forever
with those who fear him.
His salvation extends to the children's
 children
of those who are faithful to his
 covenant,
of those who obey his commandments!

Psalm 103:13–18, NLT

Marvel at God's creativity

When a newborn baby comes into the world;
when you see a rose, its petals all unfurled,
is it chance or science or the whispers of God?

Whispers of God, Marilyn Baker[4]

You made all the delicate,
  inner parts of my body
and knit me together in my
  mother's womb.

Thank you for making me so
  wonderfully complex!
Your workmanship is marvelous
  – how well I know it.

You watched me as I was being formed
  in utter seclusion,
as I was woven together
  in the dark of the womb.

You saw me before I was born.
Every day of my life was recorded
  in your book.
Every moment was laid out
  before a single day had passed.

How precious are your thoughts about me,
  O God.
They cannot be numbered!

Psalm 139:13–17, NLT

Love

Unconditional love

God's love for you is unconditional. That means He loves you, even though He has no illusions about you. He knows you at your best – and worst. Also, He knows your future. Knowing the end from the beginning doesn't alter His love for you. Ask Him to give you this gift of love for your child.

Love is not love
Which alters when it alteration finds,
Or bends with the remover to remove:

O no! it is an ever-fixed mark
That looks on tempests
*   and is never shaken ...*

'Sonnet 116', William Shakespeare, 1564?–1616

... nothing can ever separate us from God's love. Neither death nor life, neither angels nor demons, neither our fears for today nor our worries about tomorrow – not even the powers of hell can separate us from God's love. No power in the sky above or in the earth below – indeed, nothing in all creation will ever be able to separate us from the love of God that is revealed in Christ Jesus our Lord.

Romans 8:38–39, NLT

Unforgettable

Mums of newborns find it impossible to stop thinking about their babies for long. But when children become adults, many mums go on thinking and worrying about them. And even if a child is miscarried or still-born, few women forget the child they have carried, but lost. God never forgets us, His children.

Can a mother forget her nursing child?

Can she feel no love for the child she has borne?

But even if that were possible, I would not forget you!

See, I have written your name on the palms of my hands.

Isaiah 49:15–16, NLT

Love defined

What is love? Ask God for a deeper understanding of His love for you, as you learn to love your child. Let your experience as a mother change the way you love others.

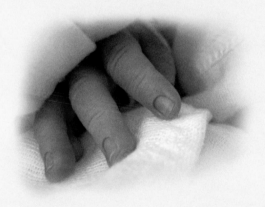

Love is patient and kind. Love is not jealous or boastful or proud or rude. It does not demand its own way. It is not irritable, and it keeps no record of being wronged. It does not rejoice about injustice but rejoices whenever the truth wins out. Love never gives up, never loses faith, is always hopeful, and endures through every circumstance.

1 Corinthians 13:4–7, NLT

Sacrificial love

I have found the paradox, that if you love until it hurts, there can be no more hurt, only more love.

Mother Teresa, 1910–1997

38

We know what real love is because Jesus gave up his life for us. So we also ought to give up our lives for our brothers and sisters. If someone has enough money to live well and sees a brother or sister in need but shows no compassion – how can God's love be in that person?

1 John 3:16–17, NLT

Concerns

Overwhelmed

Inadequate?

Watch a child being taught to swim by a loving parent and you'll catch a glimpse of Psalm 34. All the time the child knows that strong arms are there to rescue, he or she can be confident. Learning to swim can be fun. The same child, thrown into a pool alone, would be terrified, but knowing Dad or Mum is there banishes fear and instils confidence. When you feel as if you are sinking – inadequate for the task of motherhood – call out to God. Ask Him to make you aware of His loving arms ready to rescue you and carry you if necessary.

*Those who look to him for help will be
radiant with joy;
no shadow of shame will darken their
faces ...*

*Taste and see that the Lord is good.
Oh, the joys of those who take refuge in
him ...*

*The Lord hears his people when they call
to him for help.
He rescues them from all their troubles.*

*The Lord is close to the brokenhearted;
he rescues those whose spirits are
crushed.*

*The righteous person faces many troubles
but the Lord comes to the rescue each time.*

Psalm 34:5,8,17–19, NLT

43

Worried?

Night feeds can be lonely times when your emotional and spiritual defences are at their lowest. Don't fall into the trap of worrying. Focus on God's ability rather than your own anxieties and inadequacies.

> *I lie awake thinking of you,*
> *meditating on you through the night.*
> *Because you are my helper,*
> *I sing for joy in the shadow of your wings.*
> *I cling to you;*
> *your strong right hand holds me*
> *securely.*

Psalm 63:6–8, NLT

*Give all your worries and cares to God,
for he cares about you.*

1 Peter 5:7, NLT

*Rest in my love, relax in my care
And know that my presence will always
 be there.
You are my child, and I care for you,
There's nothing my love and my power
 cannot do.*

Rest in My Love, Marilyn Baker[5]

Inexperienced?

New babies don't arrive with a parents' instruction manual. In some communities, life has changed to such an extent that new parents sometimes feel isolated without the support of other mothers who have already travelled the path of parenthood. As well as building links where you can with your own family and other parents in your community, let God be your teacher. He promises to guide us.

*Trust in the L*ORD *with all your heart;*
do not depend on your own
understanding.
Seek his will in all you do,
and he will show you which path to take.

Proverbs 3:5–6, NLT

46

This is what the LORD says, he who made the earth, the LORD who formed it and established it – the LORD is his name: 'Call to me and I will answer you and tell you great and unsearchable things you do not know.'

Jeremiah 33:2–3, NIV

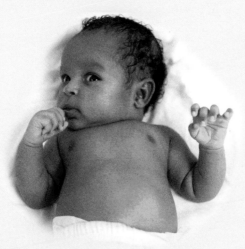

47

Weak?

Sometimes motherhood brings out unexpected attributes. The most timid woman can become a roaring lioness if her child is threatened. But even the strongest and most confident woman can feel weak in the face of the physical and emotional demands of motherhood. Here's what God says:

> *Do you have a powerful arm*
> *and a thundering voice*
> *that compare with mine?*

Job 40:9, CEV

Ouch!
Father,
why do I
strain my frail
wrists
when You offer Your
mighty arm?

Susan L. Lenzkes[6]

Exhausted

Strength renewed

God energises tired people. At times, mums find resources of seemingly super-human strength, especially when their child needs help.

God also puts us in families and communities to help each other.

If you are physically tired out by the tasks of motherhood, team up with another tired mum and take turns to have time out to regain your strength. But don't neglect to also draw on the strength God gives.

Do you not know?
Have you not heard?
The LORD is the everlasting God,
the Creator of the ends of the earth.
He will not grow tired or weary,
and his understanding no-one can
  fathom.
He gives strength to the weary
and increases the power of the weak.
Even youths grow tired and weary,
and young men stumble and fall;
but those who hope in the LORD
will renew their strength.
They will soar on wings like eagles;
they will run and not grow weary,
they will walk and not be faint.

Isaiah 40:28–31, NIV

Time out

Jesus knew about being tired. He made sure His followers had the rest they needed.

> *Then Jesus said, 'Let's go off by ourselves to a quiet place and rest awhile.' He said this because there were so many people coming and going that Jesus and his apostles didn't even have time to eat.*

Mark 6:31, NLT

52

To discover how the nights will feel, walk around the living room from 5pm to 10pm carrying a wet bag weighing 8–12 pounds. At 10pm put the bag down, set the alarm for midnight and go to sleep. Get up at midnight and walk around the living room again, with the bag, until 1am. Put the alarm on for 3am and as you can't get back to sleep, get up at 2am and make a drink. Go to bed at 2.45am, get up at 3am when the alarm goes off. Sing songs in the dark until 4am. Put the alarm on for 5am. Get up. Make breakfast. Keep this up for five years. Look cheerful.

'The Perfect Parents' Preparation Plan', Unknown

53

Go gently

Don't be hard on yourself. God
deals gently with mums like you.

*He tends his flock like a shepherd:
He gathers the lambs in his arms
and carries them close to his
heart; he gently leads those that
have young.*

Isaiah 40:11, NIV

Ask God for His strength every day, especially when you feel exhausted and need rest.

Keep your eye on me;
hide me under your cool wing feathers ...

Psalm 17:8–9, *The Message*

Reclaiming your body

As a new mum you might feel more like a feeding, cleaning machine than a desirable woman. Read Song of Songs chapter 7 and remember you are still the woman that God created.

How beautiful are your sandaled feet,
   princess!
The curves of your thighs are like
   jewelry,
the handiwork of a master.
Your navel is a rounded bowl;
it never lacks mixed wine.
Your waist is a mound of wheat
surrounded by lilies.
Your breasts are like two fawns,
twins of a gazelle …
a king could be held captive in your
   tresses.
How beautiful you are …

Song of Songs 7:1–6, HCSB

An ideal home

In years to come no-one will care if your house was a well-decorated 'ideal home'. They will notice if you have children who know they are loved and know how to love and care for others.

Babies don't care about lifestyles – they just want love.

Sue Palmer[7]

A child needs a role model, not a supermodel.

Astrid Alauda

... I tell you not to worry about everyday life – whether you have enough food and drink, or enough clothes to wear. Isn't life more than food, and your body more than clothing? Look at the birds. They don't plant or harvest or store food in barns, for your heavenly Father feeds them. And aren't you far more valuable to him than they are?

... your heavenly Father already knows all your needs. Seek the Kingdom of God above all else, and live righteously, and he will give you everything you need.

Matthew 6:25–26,32–33, NLT

Re-creation

Exhausted spiritually, don't miss out on opportunities for spiritual input. You wouldn't let your baby go hungry – but you might neglect to feed your own spirit. You and your baby will suffer. You might not have time to read or to attend lots of Christian events, but if you use the internet, you can download teaching to listen to as you are doing chores. Or, if that involves too much brain-power at this stage in life, you can play music CDs at home and in the car. Sing along – even if you don't like the sound of your own voice, the words and music will touch your spirit – and your baby's. And don't forget the renewing and re-energising potential of a (possibly child-free?) walk in the country or a picnic in a park enjoying God's creation. Give yourself permission and space to restore your spiritual batteries.

Gather the people,
consecrate the assembly;
bring together the elders,
gather the children,
those nursing at the breast …

'I am sending you grain, new wine
*   and oil,*
enough to satisfy you fully …

You will have plenty to eat, until you
*   are full,*
and you will praise the name of the
*   Lord your God,*
who has worked wonders for you;
never again will my people be shamed.'

Joel 2:16,19,26, NIV

61

Daunted

A change of pace

A new baby changes the pace of life. Although there is an endless list of tasks to be done … and done again tomorrow, those tasks can't be hurried. This is not the time in life to be snatching a quick bite to eat so you can get on with 'something important'. Take time for meals. It's OK if washing, dressing, feeding and sleeping take all day. This *is* 'something important'. The routines and bonds established now will last a lifetime.

Dressing a small child is not as easy as it seems. To practise, buy an octopus and a draw-string bag. Attempt to put the octopus into the bag so that none of the arms hang out. Time allowed: all morning.

Unknown

This is what the Sovereign Lord, the Holy One of Israel, says:
'In repentance and rest is your salvation, in quietness and trust is your strength ...'

Isaiah 30:15, NIV

One day at a time

I said to the man who stood at the gate
   of the year,
'Give me a light that I may tread safely
   into the unknown.'
And he replied, 'Go into the darkness and
   put your hand into the hand of God.
That shall be to you better than light
   and safer than a known way.'

Minnie Louise Haskins[8]

Parenthood

I searched –
but there definitely was not
a packet of instructions
attached to my children
when they arrived.
And none has since
come through my letter-box.
Lord, show me how
to be a good parent.
Teach me to
correct without crushing,
help without hanging on,
listen without laughing,
surround without smothering,
and love without limit –
the way You love me.

Susan L. Lenzkes[9]

65

The master builder

Since the creation of the world God has been bringing order and structure, beauty and new life to formless emptiness. He is with you to bring order and structure to your baby's life, bringing beauty and harmony out of what may seem to be chaos!

Afflicted city, storm-battered, unpitied:
I'm about to rebuild you with stones
*   of turquoise,*
Lay your foundations with sapphires,
construct your towers with rubies,
Your gates with jewels,
and all your walls with precious stones.
All your children will have God for
*   their teacher –*
what a mentor for your children!
You'll be built solid, grounded in
*   righteousness,*
far from any trouble – nothing to fear!
Far from terror – it won't even
*   come close!*

Isaiah 54:11–17, *The Message*

67

A bright future

Bring all your concerns and fears to God who holds the future. As Mothers' Union founder Mary Sumner once said, 'Be yourself what you wish your children to be.'

Rise during the night and cry out.
Pour out your hearts like water to
the Lord.
Lift up your hands to him in prayer,
pleading for your children ...

Lamentations 2:19, NLT

You, LORD, are all I want!
You are my choice,
and you keep me safe.
You make my life pleasant,
and my future is bright.
I praise you, LORD,
for being my guide.
Even in the darkest night,
your teachings fill my mind.
I will always look to you,
as you stand beside me
and protect me from fear.
With all my heart,
I will celebrate,
and I can safely rest.

Psalm 16:5–9, CEV

Fearful

Relax in God's love

Mums are constantly bombarded with advice: cook more veg; avoid too much TV; read more; play more; watch out for stranger danger. It is easy to become fearful, thinking, 'If I'm not a perfect parent, my child will fail.'

The Bible's antidote to fear is love. Get to know how much God loves you and your child.

Such love has no fear, because perfect love expels all fear. If we are afraid, it is for fear of punishment, and this shows that we have not fully experienced his perfect love.

1 John 4:18, NLT

*Don't be afraid, for I am with you.
Don't be discouraged, for I am
   your God.
I will strengthen you and help you.
I will hold you up with my victorious
   right hand.*

Isaiah 41:10, NLT

71

You are not alone

Hymn writer Civilla Martin visited a couple in New York in 1905 called Mr and Mrs Doolittle. She recalled:

'Mrs Doolittle had been bedridden for nigh twenty years. Her husband was an incurable cripple who had to propel himself to and from his business in a wheelchair. Despite their afflictions, they lived happy Christian lives, bringing inspiration and comfort to all who knew them. One day while we were visiting with the Doolittles, my husband commented on their bright hopefulness and asked them for the secret of it. Mrs Doolittle's reply was simple: "His eye is on the sparrow, and I know He watches me." The beauty of this simple expression of boundless faith gripped the hearts and fired the imagination of Dr. Martin and me. The hymn *His Eye is on the Sparrow* was the outcome of that experience.'[10]

Why should I feel discouraged, why should the shadows come,
Why should my heart be lonely, and long for heaven and home,
When Jesus is my portion?
My constant friend is He:
His eye is on the sparrow, and I know He watches me;
His eye is on the sparrow, and I know He watches me.

His Eye is on the Sparrow, Civilla Martin, 1866–1948

Angelic armies

Sometimes life feels like a battle ground. We are bombarded by demands on all sides. Let God shelter and protect you.

He will cover you with his feathers.
He will shelter you with his wings.
His faithful promises are your armour
    and protection.
Do not be afraid of the terrors of
    the night,
nor the arrow that flies in the day.
Do not dread the disease that stalks
    in darkness,
nor the disaster that strikes at midday.

Psalm 91:4–6, NLT

God will command his angels
to protect you
wherever you go.
They will carry you
in their arms ...

Psalm 91:11–12, CEV

You are my hiding place,
You always fill my heart
  with songs of deliverance.
Whenever I am afraid,
  I will trust in You.
I will trust in You.
Let the weak say I am strong
  In the strength of the Lord.

You are My Hiding Place, Michael Ledner[11]

Prayer battle

Do not be anxious about anything, but in everything, by prayer and petition, with thanksgiving, present your requests to God.

Philippians 4:6, NIV

Never give up praying. And when you pray, keep alert and be thankful.

Colossians 4:2, CEV

And we know that in all things God works for the good of those who love him, who have been called according to his purpose.

Romans 8:28, NIV

*Our God, you are the one
who rides on the clouds,
and we praise you.
Your name is the LORD,
and we celebrate
as we worship you.
Our God, from your sacred home
you take care of orphans
and protect widows.
You find families
for those who are lonely.*

Psalm 68:4–6, CEV

Hopes

∽

Dreams

∽

Prayers

Your newborn baby

Declare truth

Your baby is a spiritual being as well as flesh and blood. Don't wait to start talking to your baby about God. If the baby in Elizabeth's womb could leap for joy when Mary arrived, carrying Jesus the Son of God in her womb, perhaps your child can understand more than you might think! Your baby was born with a sensitive spirit.

As soon as the sound of your greeting reached my ears, the baby in my womb leaped for joy.

Luke 1:44, NIV

God has plans for your child, just as He has plans for you.

See that you do not look down on one of these little ones. For I tell you that their angels in heaven always see the face of my Father in heaven.

Matthew 18:10, NIV

But you are a chosen people, a royal priesthood, a holy nation, a people belonging to God, that you may declare the praises of him who called you out of darkness into his wonderful light.

1 Peter 2:9, NIV

Sing songs

Elderly people suffering from dementia, who forget even their own name, can sometimes remember word for word the songs they learned as children. Speech and songs are processed in different parts of the brain. Sing nursery rhymes, songs and simple choruses – accompanied by CDs if that helps you. Your child will learn lessons which will last a lifetime. Music is also a useful tool to influence your baby's mood.

Jesus loves me! This I know,
For the Bible tells me so.
Little ones to Him belong;
They are weak, but He is strong.

Yes, Jesus loves me!
Yes, Jesus loves me!
Yes, Jesus loves me!
The Bible tells me so.

Anna B. Warner, 1860

Love talking

Faith is caught not taught. Celebrate the Christian festivals. Keep Sunday special. Read the Bible and pray together as a family. Talk about what you are watching on television. Develop a Christian worldview: 'What would Jesus do or say in this situation?' Use ordinary events like cooking meals, cleaning, walking or gardening to explain Christian principles. Instill godly habits, and when your children are older they are likely to want to give their own children the same foundations.

*Listen, Israel! The L*ORD *our God is the only true God! So love the L*ORD *your God with all your heart, soul, and strength. Memorise his laws and tell them to your children over and over again. Talk about them all the time, whether you're at home or walking along the road or going to bed at night, or getting up in the morning.*

Deuteronomy 6:4–7, CEV

Pray blessings

The people brought children to Jesus, hoping he might touch them. The disciples shooed them off. But Jesus was irate and let them know it: 'Don't push these children away. Don't ever get between them and me. These children are at the very center of life in the kingdom. Mark this: Unless you accept God's kingdom in the simplicity of a child, you'll never get in.' Then, gathering the children up in his arms, he laid his hands of blessing on them.

Mark 10:13–16, *The Message*

The LORD bless you and keep you;
the LORD make his face shine upon you
and be gracious to you;
the LORD turn his face towards you
and give you peace.

'Aaron's Blessing', Numbers 6:24–26, NIV

We prayed over our children every bedtime for several years using this blessing. Our children had their own version which ended: 'The Lord will turn his plate towards you and give you his peas!'

Catherine Butcher

Your growing child

Letting go

Giving birth is the first step to letting go. It might be difficult to contemplate now, but the best parents equip their children to live independently.

I held you in my arms
At that moment there was we
Then the cord was cut
You were you and I was I
The rest of our lives is a journey of discovery
We explore, you and I
In you I see all the good and bad I have
  bequeathed you
But also the you that is totally different
  from the I
We come together in unity, bonded by
  our commonality
But also live apart, knowing
That our separateness is also a gift
The art of parenthood is to foster the new.

'To Foster the New'[12]

Training time

Children need boundaries and, although they will test the limits, they feel safest and most secure when boundaries are clearly defined and they know there will be consequences to face if they cross them. Aim to be consistently loving but firm and you will see the benefit in your children as they grow up.

> LORD, *you have assigned me my portion and my cup;*
> *you have made my lot secure.*
> *The boundary lines have fallen for me in pleasant places;*
> *surely I have a delightful inheritance.*
>
> Psalm 16:5–6, NIV

Train a child in the way he should go,
and when he is old he will not turn from it.

Proverbs 22:6, NIV

But as for you, continue in what
you have learned and have become
convinced of, because you know those
from whom you learned it, and how
from infancy you have known the holy
Scriptures, which are able to make
you wise for salvation through faith in
Christ Jesus.

2 Timothy 3:14–15, NIV

Living example

...do not exasperate your children;
instead, bring them up in the training and
instruction of the Lord.

Ephesians 6:4, NIV

The Bible says that the disciples were
approached by some Greek people who said,
'We would like to see Jesus' (John 12:20–22,
NIV). Your children also need to see Jesus.
Although they can't see Him physically, you
are their example. Let this be your prayer:

Let the beauty of Jesus be seen in me
All His wonderful passion and purity
O my Saviour divine, all my being refine
Till the beauty of Jesus be seen in me.

Albert Orsborn, 1886–1967

A mother is the truest friend we have, when trials, heavy and sudden, fall upon us; when adversity takes the place of prosperity; when friends who rejoice with us in our sunshine, desert us when troubles thicken around us, still will she cling to us, and endeavor by her kind precepts and counsels to dissipate the clouds of darkness, and cause peace to return to our hearts.

Washington Irving[13]

Each day of our lives we make deposits in the memory banks of our children.

Charles (Chuck) Swindoll[14]

The family should be a closely knit group. The home should be a self-contained shelter of security; a kind of school where life's basic lessons are taught; and a kind of church where God is honored; a place where wholesome recreation and simple pleasures are enjoyed.

Billy Graham, 'My Answer' syndicated newspaper column[15]

Lessons for life

Children can recover quickly from the bumps and scrapes of childhood rough and tumble. But a wounded heart can leave a child emotionally scarred. Guard your child's heart. You can't be with your child in every situation but bedtime is a good opportunity to talk about the day and how they felt. Some children need extra help to articulate feelings. Be open about how you feel in different situations and how God has helped you. Give them the vocabulary to air their feelings and teach them to use the armour described in Ephesians 6:10–18 to protect themselves emotionally and spiritually.

Be ready! Let the truth be like a belt around your waist, and let God's justice protect you like armour. Your desire to tell the good news about peace should be like shoes on your feet. Let your faith be like a shield, and you will be able to stop all the flaming arrows of the evil one. Let God's saving power be like a helmet, and for a sword use God's message that comes from the Spirit.

Never stop praying, especially for others. Always pray by the power of the Spirit. Stay alert and keep praying for God's people.

Ephesians 6:14–18, CEV

Looking ahead

Knowing God

Pray for your children's future. God willing, they will become adults and take their place in the world.

God has already taken the initiative, putting a longing for eternity in their hearts (Ecclesiastes 3:11).

Make Paul's prayer for the Ephesians a prayer for your child:

> *For this reason I kneel before the Father, from whom his whole family in heaven and on earth derives its name. I pray that out of his glorious riches he may strengthen you with power through his Spirit in your inner being, so that Christ may dwell in your hearts through faith. And I pray that you, being rooted and established in love, may have power, together with all the saints, to grasp how wide and long and high and deep is the love of Christ, and to know this love that surpasses knowledge – that you may be filled to the measure of all the fullness of God.*

Ephesians 3:14–19, NIV

This is a verse I chose especially for my daughter, Rachel ...

Above all else, guard your heart,
for it is the wellspring of life.

Proverbs 4:23, NIV

... and a special verse for my son, Matthew:

Be strong and courageous. Do not be afraid
... for the LORD your God goes with you; he will
never leave you nor forsake you.

Deuteronomy 31:6, NIV

... and a verse from a psalm, with some extra words
added, for our whole family ...

I can lie down
and sleep soundly
because you, LORD,
will keep me [and my family] safe.

Psalm 4:8, CEV

Catherine Butcher

Becoming wise

You may not be able to give your children an inheritance of worldly wealth, but make sure you live wisely and pass on an inheritance that lasts.

Listen, [my] sons, to a father's discipline,
and pay attention so that you may gain
understanding,
for I am giving you good instruction.
Don't abandon my teaching.
When I was a son with my father,
tender and precious to my mother,
he taught me and said:
'Your heart must hold on to my words.
Keep my commands and live.
Get wisdom, get understanding;
don't forget or turn away from the words
of my mouth.'

Proverbs 4:1–5, HCSB

Build on firm foundations

The children's song based on the Parable of the Wise
and Foolish Builders in Matthew 7:24–27 makes a
great action song to teach children, who love the
'splat'. It also teaches truth – wise people build their
lives on firm foundations so that when troubles come
they can stand strong:

> *The wise man built his house upon the rock ...*
> *The rain came down ...*
> *And the floods came up ...*
> *And the house on the rock stood firm.*

In contrast:

> *The foolish man built his house upon the sand ...*
> *The rain came down ...*
> *And the floods came up ...*
> *And the house on the sand went 'splat!'*

Unknown

99

Hearing God's voice

In the Old Testament story of Hannah, her longed-for son Samuel was born after fervent prayer. She could have held on to him, but she gave him back to God and Samuel grew up serving God in the Temple, which is where he first learned to recognise God's voice. The story is in 1 Samuel.

Hannah said:

> *'I prayed for this child, and the LORD has granted me what I asked of him.'*

1 Samuel 1:27, NIV

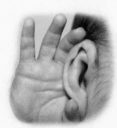

Pray that your child also learns to hear from God.

*Now Samuel did not yet know the L*ORD*: The word of the L*ORD *had not yet been revealed to him.*

*The L*ORD *called Samuel a third time, and Samuel got up and went to Eli and said, 'Here I am; you called me.'*

*Then Eli realised that the L*ORD *was calling the boy. So Eli told Samuel, 'Go and lie down, and if he calls you, say, "Speak, L*ORD*, for your servant is listening."' So Samuel went and lay down in his place.*

*The L*ORD *came and stood there, calling as at the other times, 'Samuel! Samuel!'*

Then Samuel said, 'Speak, for your servant is listening.'

1 Samuel 3:7–10, NIV

Always welcome home

You're never too old to be my son,
You're never so disobedient that my
compassion ends,
You're never so far away that you can't turn
around and come home.

'Grown-up Children?', Valerie Brown[16]

Where can I go from your Spirit?
Where can I flee from your presence?
If I go up to the heavens, you are there;
if I make my bed in the depths, you are there.
If I rise on the wings of the dawn,
if I settle on the far side of the sea,
even there your hand will guide me,
your right hand will hold me fast.

Psalm 139:7–10, NIV

Like the father in the parable of the Prodigal Son, always be ready to welcome your children back, no matter how far they have strayed.

But while he [the son] was still a long way off, his father saw him and was filled with compassion for him; he ran to his son, threw his arms around him and kissed him.

Luke 15:20, NIV

Live well

Inspire

Try and live in such a way that your children may be proud of you.

*Children's children are a crown
to the aged,
and parents are the pride of
their children.*

Proverbs 17:6, NIV

A role model to aspire to!

She watches over the affairs of
   her household
and does not eat the bread
   of idleness.

Her children arise and call her
   blessed;
her husband also, and he
   praises her:

'Many women do noble things,
but you surpass them all.'

Proverbs 31:27–29, NIV

Happy families

God can take the most damaged person and bring healing, but a good start in life, with balanced, loving parents does help.

Parents who love each other give an invaluable, lasting legacy to a child, who will watch them to learn how to love, resolve conflict, forgive, share and reach agreements.

Your own well-being and that of your baby's father are important. Ask a friend or relative to care for your baby for a few hours every week, so you can rest, recover and enjoy each other's company as adults, not just as parents. If you are a lone-parent, find a support network where you can enjoy adult company as a person in your own right, not only as your baby's mother.

As far as you are able, keep good communication channels with your children.

> *Make a clean sweep of malice and pretense, envy and hurtful talk. You've had a taste of God. Now, like infants at the breast, drink deep of God's pure kindness. Then you'll grow up mature and whole in God.*

1 Peter 2:1–3, *The Message*

Definition of 'grandparents': The people who think your children are wonderful even though they're sure you're not raising them right.

Living together in peace

It is truly wonderful
when relatives live together
in peace.
It is as beautiful as olive oil
poured on Aaron's head and running
  down his beard
and the collar of his robe.
It is like the dew
from Mount Hermon,
falling on Zion's mountains,
*where the L*ord *has promised*
to bless his people
with life forevermore.

Psalm 133, CEV

God is the one who makes us patient and cheerful. I pray that he will help you live at peace with each other, as you follow Christ. Then all of you together will praise God, the Father of our Lord Jesus Christ.

Romans 15:5–6, CEV

A global perspective

Help your children to be aware of others and their needs. Be inclusive when you hold family gatherings, involving single people and others who might spend most of their leisure time alone. Your children will benefit from being part of an extended family.

It takes a village to raise a child.

African proverb

Encourage your children to take their place in the world, aware of those who have less than they do.

Almighty One, we praise you and give thanks for life, and for all children who start life in innocence, laughter and play. Make us mindful of the world's children in the name of your beloved Son, who took them into his arms and blessed them. Grant us grace to embrace these little ones with nurturing love, to promote their strong physical growth, so that they may develop with keen minds and lively hearts. Awaken our consciences and lead us, we pray, to recognise, acknowledge and repent of our collusion that has caused their suffering – their hunger, thirst, sickness and early death. Give us holy anger and stir our wills and hearts to act on their behalf, for the sake of your love. Amen.

'To Act on Their Behalf', Jessica A. Hatch[17]

Notes

Thanks

1. *Common Worship*, Thanksgiving for the Gift of a Child. Extracts from *Common Worship* are copyright © The Archbishops' Council and are reproduced by permission.

2. *Common Worship*, Thanksgiving for the Gift of a Child. Extracts from *Common Worship* are copyright © The Archbishops' Council and are reproduced by permission.

3. Anne E. Kitch, from Abigail Nelson *et al.*, eds.,*Lifting women's voices – prayers to change the world*. Extracts from *Lifting women's voices* are reproduced in the UK by permission of Canterbury Press. Elsewhere, ©2009 the Domestic and Foreign Ministry. All rights reserved. Used by permission of Church Publishing Incorporated, New York, NY. p.210.

4. Marilyn Baker, *Whispers of God*. from *From The Beginning* on the *Ultimate Collection* © 1981 Authentic Publishing. Used by permission.

Concerns

5. Marilyn Baker, *Rest in My Love*. Copyright © 1987 Authentic Publishing/kingswaysongs.com. Used by permission.

6. Susan L. Lenzkes, *When the Handwriting on the Wall is in Brown Crayon* (Farnham, CWR, 1974) p.74.

7. Sue Palmer, *Toxic Childhood* (London: Orion) in an interview for *Families First* magazine.

8. Minnie Louise Haskins wrote the poem in 1908. It was used by King George VI in his Christmas message broadcast in 1939 at the beginning of the Second World War.

9. Susan L. Lenzkes, op.cit. p.18.

10. Quotation from website: http://www.hymntime.com/tch/htm/h/i/hiseyeis.htm

11. Michael Ledner, *You are My Hiding Place* © 1981 CCCM Music/Maranatha! Music. Administered by Song Solutions Copycare, 14 Horsted Square, Uckfield TN22 1QG, info@songsolutions.org. Used by permission.

12. Author unknown, from Abigail Nelson *et al.*, eds., *Lifting women's voices – prayers to change the world,* op. cit.

Hopes, dreams and prayers

13. Source: www.thoughts-about-God.com/quotes/quotes-mothers.htm

14. Source: Insight for Living http://dailychristianquote.com/dcqfamily.html

15. Source: 'My Answer' syndicated newspaper column

16. Source: Scripture Union 'WordLive' website, http://www.scriptureunion.org.uk/2981.id?sessionid=14300&activityid=74355

17. From Abigail Nelson *et al.*, eds., *Lifting women's voices – prayers to change the world*. op. cit.